How to Draw
South Carolina's
Sights and Symbols

Eric Fein

The Rosen Publishing Group's
PowerKids Press™
New York

Published in 2002 by The Rosen Publishing Group, Inc.
29 East 21st Street, New York, NY 10010

First Edition

Editors: Jennifer Landau, Jennifer Way
Book and Layout Design: Kim Sonsky

Illustration Credits: Jamie Grecco
Photo Credits: p. 7 © National Gallery Collection; by kind permission of the Trustees of the National Gallery, London/CORBIS; p. 8 © Marie Danforth Paige/© Tradd Street Press; p. 9 © Gibbes Museum of Art/Carolina Art Association; pp. 12, 14 © One Mile Up, Inc.; p. 16 © Hal Horwitz/CORBIS; p. 18 © Raymond Gehman/CORBIS; p. 20 © Mary Ann McDonald/CORBIS; p. 22 © Joe McDonald; p. 24 © William A. Bake/CORBIS; p. 26 © Bettmann/CORBIS; p. 28 © Index Stock.

Fein, Eric
        How to draw South Carolina's sights and symbols / Eric Fein.
            p. cm. — (A kid's guide to drawing America)
        Includes index.
        Summary: This book explains how to draw some of South Carolina's sights and symbols, including the state seal, the official flower, and the USS Yorktown, an aircraft carrier docked in Mount Pleasant, South Carolina.
        ISBN 0-8239-6097-8
        1. Emblems, State—South Carolina—Juvenile literature   2. South Carolina—In art—Juvenile literature
3. Drawing—Technique—Juvenile literature
[1. Emblems, State—South Carolina   2. South Carolina   3. Drawing—Technique]   I. Title
II. Series
        743'.8'99757—dc21

Manufactured in the United States of America

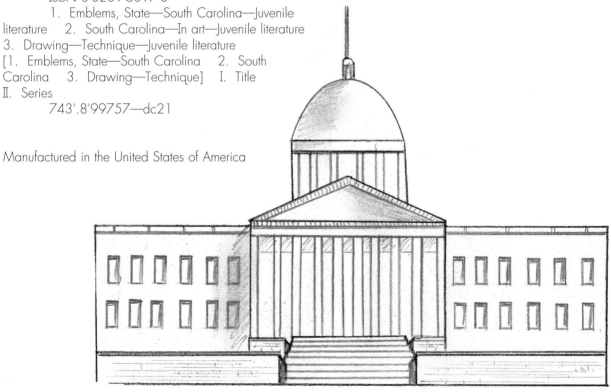

CONTENTS

Let's Draw South Carolina

South Carolina is one of the smallest states of the South. Don't let its size fool you, though. South Carolina has played important roles in the American Revolution (1775–1783) and the Civil War (1861–1865).

Two-thirds of South Carolina is covered by forests. The state has two national forests, Francis Marion, which is near Charleston, and Sumter, which runs through the Piedmont and the Blue Ridge Mountains areas. South Carolina also has 47 state parks and historic sites. Charles Towne Landing is where the first English settlement was established. Kings Mountain National Military Park is located near Blacksburg and is the site of a major Revolutionary War battle, in which American patriots defeated American loyalists in 1780.

Today vacationers flock to South Carolina's beautiful Myrtle Beach for swimming and sunbathing. Myrtle Beach gets its name from the wax myrtle, which is a shrub that grows all around that area. South Carolina is also known for its gardens. The Middleton Gardens have flowers and trees from all around the world. They are also the oldest landscaped gardens in the United States. The state also hosts many sporting events, including the Carolina Cup Steeplechase and the Southern 500 stock car race.

This book will help you learn to draw some of South Carolina's most fascinating sights and symbols. In each chapter, you will find step-by-step instructions showing you how to draw the subject of that chapter. Each drawing is broken down into several easy-to-follow steps. The new drawing step is shown in red.

You will need the following supplies to draw South Carolina's sights and symbols:

- A sketch pad
- An eraser
- A number 2 pencil
- A pencil sharpener

These are some of the shapes and drawing terms you need to know to draw South Carolina's sights and symbols:

3-D box		Shading	
Almond shape		Squiggle	
Horizontal line		Teardrop	
Oval		Vertical line	
Rectangle		Wavy line	

The Palmetto State

South Carolina gets its name from the Latin word *Carolus*, which means "Charles." The state was named for King Charles I of England.

In 1629, King Charles I granted land, which included the future state of South Carolina, to Sir Robert Heath. Heath did nothing with it. In 1663, King Charles II gave the South Carolina region to eight English noblemen. In 1670, they sent people to establish an English settlement in South Carolina. By the 1760s, Parliament raised taxes so much that the colonies fought back against England. This is what started the American Revolution (1775–1783). British forces attacked the city of Charleston. The colonists were able to defeat them during the Battle of Sullivan's Island, at Fort Moultrie. Fort Moultrie was made from palmetto logs. The logs were able to hold up against the British cannonballs! This is where South Carolina got its nickname, the Palmetto State.

South Carolina became the eighth state of the United States on May 23, 1788.

South Carolina is named for King Charles I of England (pictured). He granted a tract of land to Sir Robert Heath. Part of this land later became the state of South Carolina.

South Carolina Artist

Elizabeth O'Neill Verner was born in Charleston, South Carolina, on December 21, 1883. As a teenager, she painted city scenes of Charleston in a studio she had in the rear of her parents' house.

Elizabeth O'Neill Verner

Verner went to the Pennsylvania Academy of Fine Arts from 1901 to 1903. There she studied with painter Thomas Anshutz, who had been a student of Thomas Eakins's. Eakins was a noted painter of the realist school. Realist painters show subjects as they really look. It was this style that captured Verner's imagination.

Verner began to etch in the early 1920s. Etching is a form of art that involves creating a design on a metal plate with the use of acid. The acid etches, or eats away at, the exposed metal to create imprints in the plate. Prints from the etched plate are created by using a special press and paper. The press forces ink, which has been poured into the etching, onto the paper.

By 1937, Verner began to work in pastels. Pastels are powdered pigments that range from pale to deep colors. The main subjects of Verner's pastel drawings were the African American women who sold flowers on the streets of Charleston. Verner's paintings showed these women with respect and captured their grace and dignity. She also did pastels of many South Carolinian landscapes.

Verner died in 1979 at age 95. Her paintings continue to draw new fans.

Elizabeth O'Neill Verner's *Avenue at the Oaks, Goose Creek,* is an example of her later work with pastels. She was greatly influenced by realist painters. This pastel-on-silk work was done around 1953 and measures 25" x 30" (63.5 x 76 cm).

Map of South Carolina

Map of the Continental United States

South Carolina is bordered by North Carolina and Georgia. The Atlantic Ocean borders the state on its east and southeast sides. South Carolina covers 31,189 square miles (80, 779 sq km). The highest point in the state is Sassafras Mountain. It reaches 3,560 feet (1,085 m) above sea level.

South Carolina has three land regions. They are the Atlantic Coastal Plain, the Piedmont, and the Blue Ridge Mountains. The Atlantic Coastal Plain is a lowland that covers the southeastern part of the state. The Piedmont is hilly and covers most of northwestern South Carolina. The Blue Ridge Mountains are in northwestern South Carolina. This is a protected wilderness and is also a recreational area.

1

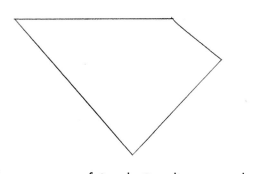

To draw a map of South Carolina, start by drawing a slanted rectangle. Notice that this shape looks like a triangle with a corner cut off.

2

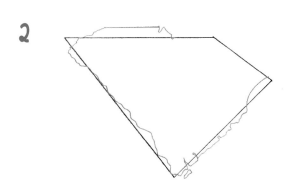

Using this shape as a guide, use squiggly lines to draw the shape of South Carolina.

3

Erase extra lines. Draw a circle for Charleston and an irregular shape for Lake Moultrie.

4

Draw slanted lines on Hilton Head Island. Add a squiggly line for the Great Pee Dee River.

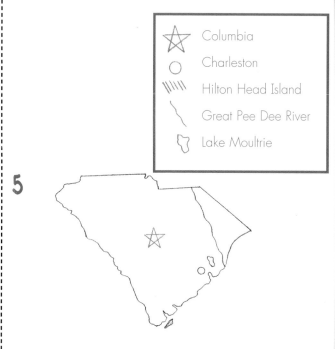

☆	Columbia
○	Charleston
\\\\\\	Hilton Head Island
∿	Great Pee Dee River
⬠	Lake Moultrie

5

Draw a star for Columbia, the capital of South Carolina, and you're done.

The State Seal

South Carolina's state seal uses two pictures to represent the Battle of Fort Moultrie on Sullivan's Island. This Revolutionary War battle took place on June 28, 1776.

The left picture shows a palmetto tree rising above a fallen oak tree. The shields on the palmetto's trunk read 4 July 1776, which is the date of the Declaration of Independence, and 26 March 1776, which is the date that South Carolina adopted its state constitution. The Latin phrase around the picture, *Animis Opibusque Parati* means "prepared in mind and resources." This is one of South Carolina's state mottoes.

The right picture shows a woman, who represents hope overcoming danger. Around this picture is the state's other motto, *Dum Spiro Spero*, which is Latin for, "While I breathe, I hope."

1

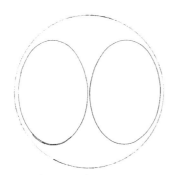

Let's draw South Carolina's seal. Begin by drawing a large circle with two ovals inside.

2

Add an oval for the woman's head and a rectangle for the tree.

3

Add a triangle as a guide for the woman's body. Add palm leaves on the tree using many crooked lines. You may also refer to the sabal palmetto drawing on page 19.

4

Carefully draw the woman's body. Notice the folds of her robe.

5

Erase the guide lines on the woman's body. Add a rectangle for the banner at the bottom of the tree. Draw the branches on the inside of the circle. The branches can be made using curved lines. The leaves can be made using almond shapes.

6

Add shading and detail, and you're done!

The State Flag

The design of South Carolina's state flag dates from 1765. Elements of the current flag were first seen on a banner carried by South Carolinian colonists. The banner used then had three white crescents against a blue background. Ten years later, in 1775, the South Carolina Revolutionary Council of Safety asked Colonel William Moultrie to design a banner that could be used by South Carolinian troops. Colonel Moultrie decided to use a simple design that had one crescent against a blue field.

A new design was ordered in 1861, when South Carolina seceded, or withdrew, from the United States at the beginning of the Civil War. This new flag kept Moultrie's design but added a palmetto tree to the center of the flag. This is the flag design used today.

1

Start by drawing a large rectangle for the flag's field.

2

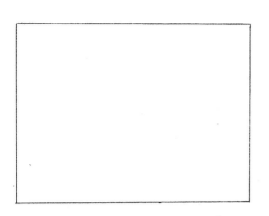

Add two circles for the moon. Notice where the edges of the circles overlap.

3

Erase extra lines. Add a triangle for the trunk of the tree.

4

Add the base of the tree's trunk. Add detail to the tree's trunk using triangles.

5

Add palm leaves to the tree using crooked lines. You may also refer to the sabal palmetto drawing on page 19.

6

Erase extra lines, and you're done. Wonderful work!

The Yellow Jessamine

In 1923, South Carolina's government formed a group to select a flower to represent the state. The committee quickly discovered that the yellow jessamine (*Gelsemium sempervirens*) was very popular with the people of South Carolina. The yellow jessamine had no competition and was declared the official state flower on February 1, 1924. The yellow jessamine grows all over the state. Its appearance signals the coming of spring.

The yellow jessamine is a climbing green vine plant, which grows up trees and along fences. It is a type of jasmine. The yellow jessamine has many yellow, trumpet-shaped flowers. These flowers are about 1 inch (2.5 cm) across and smell like true jasmine. Yellow jessamines are easy to grow and are used to decorate homes and gardens.

1

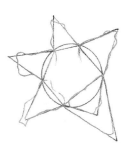

To draw the yellow jessamine, start by drawing a circle for the center of the flower.

2

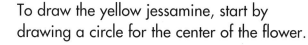

Add a triangle for the body of the flower. Notice that the bottom of the triangle is curved, rather than straight.

3

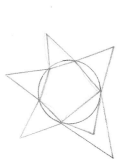

Draw five triangles around the circle. These will guide you in drawing the yellow jessamine's petals.

4

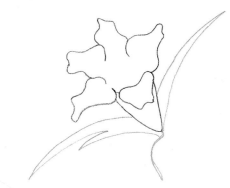

Using the triangles as guides, draw in the shape of the petals using squiggly lines. Draw the curved line for the rounded end of the flower's body.

5

Erase extra lines. Draw thin, curved triangles for the leaves. You can also add a thin, curved stem.

6

Add shading and detail to your flower, and you're done.

The Sabal Palmetto

The sabal palmetto was made South Carolina's official state tree on March 17, 1939. The tree's long history in South Carolina dates from the American Revolution. Fort Moultrie, on Sullivan's Island, was built of palmetto logs. The British soldiers were defeated by the colonial soldiers at the fort. The tree is also featured on the state flag and the state seal.

Sabal palmetto trees grow along South Carolina's coast. The tree can grow to be 80 feet (24 m) tall. The tree's large top is made of palmate leaves. Palmate leaves look like the palm sides of open hands.

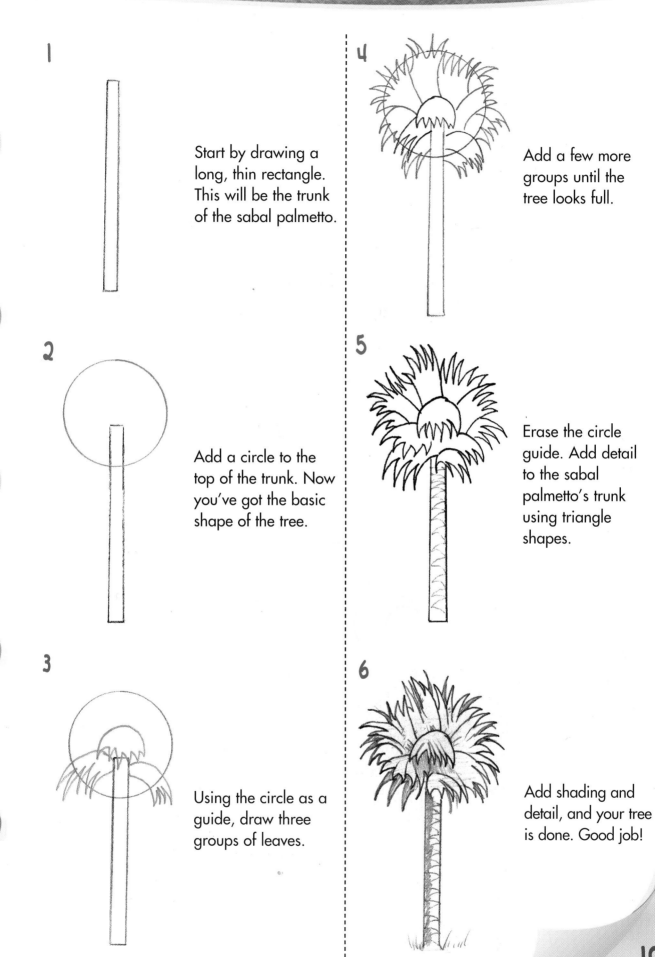

1

Start by drawing a long, thin rectangle. This will be the trunk of the sabal palmetto.

2

Add a circle to the top of the trunk. Now you've got the basic shape of the tree.

3

Using the circle as a guide, draw three groups of leaves.

4

Add a few more groups until the tree looks full.

5

Erase the circle guide. Add detail to the sabal palmetto's trunk using triangle shapes.

6

Add shading and detail, and your tree is done. Good job!

The Carolina Wren

The Carolina wren (*Thryothorus ludovicianus*) became the official state bird of South Carolina in 1948. The Carolina wren can be found all over South Carolina, from the coast to the mountains. They are even featured on the state's license plates.

The Carolina wren is 5 ½ inches (14 cm) tall and has a wingspan of 7 ½ inches (19 cm). Carolina wrens have thin bills. They have yellowish white stripes that run above their eyes. Their backs are rust brown and their bellies are dull yellow. Their tails are barred, or striped, with black. Carolina wrens make their nests in dead trees or in fence posts. They eat insects, including flies, grasshoppers, and bees. They also eat spiders, sunflower seeds, and peanuts.

1

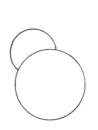

Draw two circles for the rough shape of the Carolina wren. Notice that these circles overlap.

2

Connect the circles to form the shape of the bird's body. Notice the small hump on the larger circle.

3

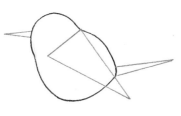

Erase extra lines, and add three triangles. These shapes will be your guides for drawing the bird's beak, its tail, and its wing.

4

Draw the beak, the tail, and the wing using curved lines. Erase extra lines, and draw the bird's legs and feet.

5

Add a circle for the eye and two wavy lines for the Carolina wren's perch, or branch.

6

Add shading and detail. Smudging your lines makes the shading look more real. Great work!

The Spotted Salamander

The spotted salamander owes its place as South Carolina's state amphibian to a third-grade class. They discovered that South Carolina did not have an official state amphibian. The class researched amphibians and asked third graders all over the state to vote for the state amphibian. The spotted salamander received the most votes. The South Carolina legislature made this the official state amphibian on May 14, 1998.

Spotted salamanders have yellow spots that run in two rows along their backs. The dorsal, or back, color of the spotted salamander is usually black. They live in forests and breed in ponds. Female spotted salamanders lay their eggs in clumps, which can contain up to 300 eggs!

1

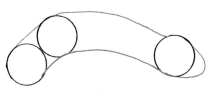

To draw the spotted salamander, begin by drawing three circles.

2

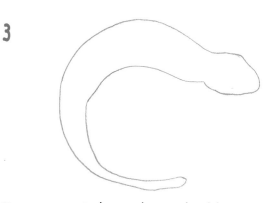

Connect your circles to form the rough shape of the body. Add a bump where the nose will be.

3

Erase your circle guides and add a curved shape for the tail.

4

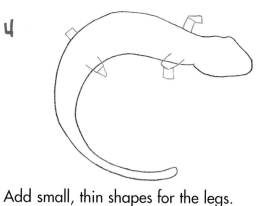

Add small, thin shapes for the legs.

5

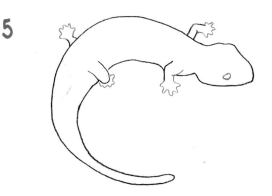

Draw a circle for the eye. Add feet and toes to each leg.

6

Add shading and detail to your spotted salamander. Notice the positions of the spots on its back. Nice work!

23

Fort Sumter

Fort Sumter is located in the harbor of Charleston, South Carolina. It was the site of the first shot fired in the Civil War. The United States split in half after the election of 1860. The Northern and Southern states each had different opinions about slavery. The Northern states remained in the Union. The Southern states seceded, or separated, to form the Confederacy. South Carolina was the first state to secede from the Union.

For a 15-month period between 1863 and 1864, Fort Sumter was under constant attack from Union soldiers. On February 17, 1865, the Union army overtook the fort. Fort Sumter became a national monument in 1948.

1

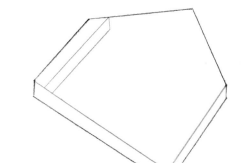

Start by drawing the basic shape of Fort Sumter.

2

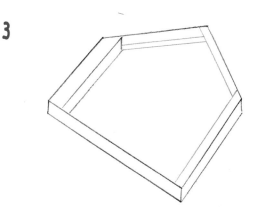

Add three rectangles for buildings and walls. This will give your drawing a 3-D look.

3

Add four more rectangles to your drawing, noting their placement on the page. These are the fort's outer walls.

4

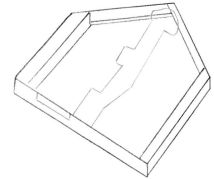

Add a rectangle along the wall, and carefully draw the center part of the fort.

5

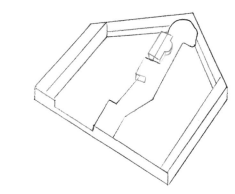

Erase extra lines. Add the two buildings in the center using rectangles. Notice that one has a curved side.

6

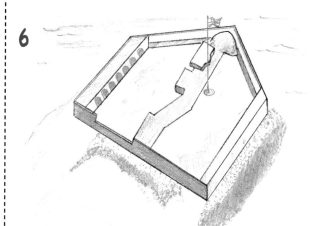

Draw rocks, a flag, and water around Fort Sumter. Add shading and detail, and you're done.

USS *Yorktown*

The USS *Yorktown* is a National Historic Landmark. The ship is docked in Mount Pleasant, South Carolina. The *Yorktown* is an aircraft carrier. It is able to carry 90 aircraft. The *Yorktown* is 856 feet (261 m) long and 93 feet (28 m) wide.

The ship was named for another ship, also called the USS *Yorktown*. That ship was sunk during the Battle of Midway in 1942, during World War II (1939–1945). The *Yorktown* was decommissioned, or taken out of service, in 1970.

Today the USS *Yorktown* offers many exhibits of what daily life is like for those serving on an aircraft carrier. It is also home to memorials that honor the memory of the people who fought and died in World War II.

1

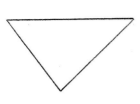

Start by drawing a triangle.

2

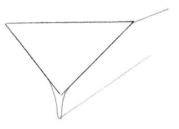

Add a round edge to the bottom of the triangle for the hull, or frame. Draw two lines along the sides to make your drawing look solid.

3

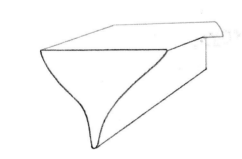

Finish the shape of the USS *Yorktown* by completing the flat deck area along the top of the ship. Erase extra lines.

4

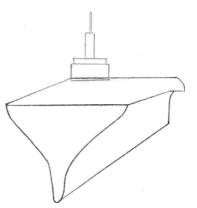

Add four rectangles for the ship's tower and a straight line for the antenna.

5

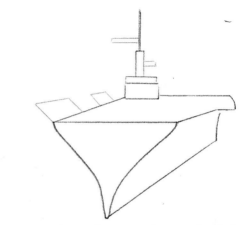

Draw two slanted rectangles on the left side of the ship, and add two more rectangles to the tower.

6

Draw water around the ship. Add shading and detail, and you're done.

South Carolina's Capitol

South Carolina's state capitol building is in Columbia, the state's capital city. It took 56 years, from 1851 to 1907, and many different architects to complete the task. The first architect, P. H. Hammerskold, did poor work and the building was torn down. He was replaced by Major John R. Niernsee. He drew up a new, Corinthian style design for the building. Corinthian style architecture is known for its highly decorated columns. Construction of this building began in 1855.

Work was stopped again during the Civil War. Other architects worked on the building until 1904, when Charles C. Wilson was chosen to finish the project. The capitol was completed in 1907.

1

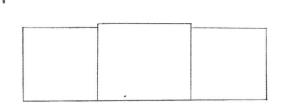

Start by drawing three rectangles.

2

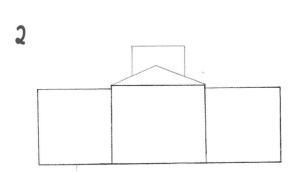

Add a triangle to the top of the middle rectangle. This triangle is called a pediment. Draw a rectangle for the base of the dome.

3

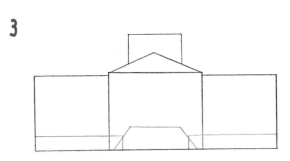

Add two rectangles along the bottom of the building. Make a slanted rectangle in the middle rectangle for the stairs.

4

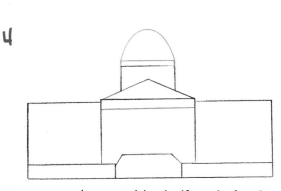

Erase extra lines. Add a half circle for the dome and two thin rectangles as details to the dome and to the pediment.

5

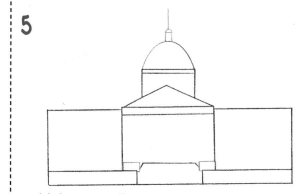

Add three small rectangles to finish the top of the dome. Draw a small rectangle on either side of the stairs.

6

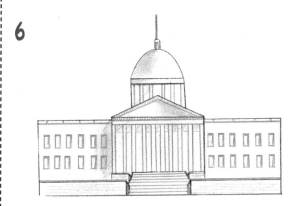

Draw the windows and the columns using thin rectangles. Add shading and detail to your building, and you're done.

South Carolina State Facts

Statehood	May 23, 1788, 8th state
Area	31,189 square miles (80, 779 sq km)
Population	3,836,000
Capital	Columbia, population, 112,800
Most Populated City	Columbia
Industries	Textile goods, chemical products, paper products, machinery, tourism
Agriculture	Tobacco, poultry, cattle, dairy products, soybeans, hogs
Animal	White-tailed deer
Song	"Carolina"
Bird	Carolina wren
Flower	Yellow jessamine
Amphibian	Spotted salamander
Tree	Sabal palmetto
Gemstone	Amethyst
Fish	Striped bass
Nickname	The Palmetto State
Mottoes	While I Breathe, I Hope and Prepared In Soul And Resources
Reptile	Loggerhead turtle

Glossary

American Revolution (uh-MER-uh-ken reh-vuh-LOO-shun) Battles that soldiers from the colonies fought against England for freedom.

architecture (AR-kih-tek-chur) The science, art, or profession of designing buildings.

Civil War (SIH-vul WOR) The war fought between the northern and southern states of America from 1861 to 1865.

Confederate (kun-FEH-duh-ret) Relating to the group of people who made up the Confederate States of America.

crescents (KREH-sents) Curved shapes.

decommissioned (dee-kuh-MIH-shund) Officially taken out of service.

dorsal (DOR-suhl) The back side of an animal.

etch (EHCH) To make a design by cutting into a material, for example, with acid.

legislature (LEH-jihs-lay-cher) A body of persons that has the power to make or pass laws.

lowland (LOH-land) Low, or level, areas of land.

motto (MAH-toh) A short sentence or phrase that says what someone believes or what something stands for.

palmate (PAHL-mayt) Resembling a hand with spread fingers.

pastels (pa-STELZ) Drawings made using pastes made of pigments.

pigments (PIG-mehnts) Coloring materials used to make pastels.

sea level (SEE LEH-vul) A way to measure how high or low something is on Earth's surface.

seceded (sih-SEED-id) Withdrew from a group or a country.

steeplechase (STEE-puhl-chays) A cross-country horse race.

Union (YOON-yun) The northern states that stayed loyal to the federal government during the Civil War.

World War II (WURLD WOR TOO) The war fought from 1939 to 1945. The United States, Great Britain, the Soviet Union, and their allies were on one side. Germany, Italy, Japan, and their allies were on the other side.

Index

Web Sites

To learn more about the people and places of South Carolina,
check out these Web sites:
http://sciway.net/facts/
www.myscgov.com/SCSGPortal/static/home_tem1.html
www.50states.com/scarolin.htm